First across the Line

and fifty other poems

Kevin Pyne

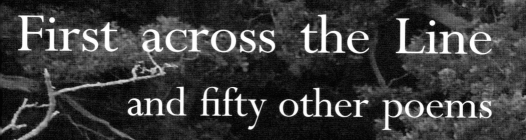

First across the Line

and fifty other poems

Kevin Pyne

Richard
Webb

AUTHOR'S DEDICATION

To Clare together with hers and mine.
Moving past your past is never easy.

Published in the United Kingdom in 2005 by Richard Webb

Designed by Laurence Daeche, Anon Design Co., Christchurch, Dorset

A CIP catalogue record for this book is available from the British Library

ISBN 0-9536361-4-3

Typeset in 14/14pt Perpetua

Printed and bound in the United Kingdom by Short Run Press, Exeter, Devon

RW.UK Ltd trading as Richard Webb, Publisher

Richard Webb, Publisher
Dartmouth, Devon, England

Kevin Pyne was born in Dartmouth, Devon in 1950. His father was from an old Dartmouth family, his mother from County Sligo, Ireland and he has two sisters. Educated at St. Cuthbert Mayne, Torquay, Kevin left school at 16 and has since worked as a boatman and ferryman on the river Dart for over 35 years.

Having to leave the ferry due to an accident at work, Kevin turned his attention to helping found the Dart Gig Club and is now an umpire on the Cornish pilot gig circuit.

He has combined this with a love of photography and has a reputation for his fine rowing pictures which, in addition to the Westcountry, he has taken in the USA, France, Holland and the Isles of Scilly.

Kevin's life has always been on or near the water and he has a special attachment to all the ports and harbours of the Westcountry and respects all those who make their living from the sea.

After nearly 30 years of marriage Kevin was widowed in 1999 when his brave and beautiful wife Lyzie died of cancer, aged only 46. Their two children are both Maritime Business graduates of the University of Plymouth – Ross is now a chartered shipbroker and Robyn is studying for her Ph.D.

Misfortune struck Kevin again in 2002 when he nearly died from the life-threatening flesh-eating disease, necrotising fasciitis, which has left him partly disabled.

After his six months in hospital he became a founder member of the Devon flag group and this green flag with a white cross can now be seen flying proudly all over Devon, like its black and white counterpart in Cornwall, both counties being part of the ancient Celtic kingdom of Dumnonia.

Kevin's experiences of observing the ever-changing life on the river, his love of the people and history of the Westcountry, the tragic loss of his wife and his own brush with death, have all shaped and coloured the many varied poems that appeared in his first work *Further up the River* which was published in 2004. *First across the Line* continues these themes.

5

PREFACE

At first I thought, foolishly, I could try to write a book of poems that made no reference to my late wife Lyzie. It's now six years or so since her death and I thought that I could move on. In truth I can't. If I am honest with myself I don't actually want to. I need to report in. Lyzie was a part of my life for thirty years so she stays forever. If I look at my daughter Robyn I am looking at her. Where did my son Ross get his organisational skills I wonder? It certainly wasn't from me. I still sense her there. My poems still scurry back into where it is that I feel safe and where I can identify with my past. If it will ever be possible to move past my emotions I'm not sure. They say we all of us have the baggage of past lives around us when we reach our fifties. I wonder why then should I be any different? I write in a sense about that baggage. I actually like writing poems which I know are for those who have been bereaved and I hope that in some way my poems have a supportive sentiment. I still feel a sense of disbelief for the cruel and unjust way in which Lyzie died.

Water and the people of the water are such a part 'of my life; it is a medium where all the people I want to be around are to be found. It's hardly surprising that it features so much in my poems and in my life. Water has now brought me another close friend.

I truly think that there are many things worse than my situation. I had all the love there was in our relationship. To have loved someone so much and lost them to another in many ways must be worse.

It might be sensible to broaden out my poems so that I encompass everyone and make all my readers feel that I write for all of them. I am, though, a Westcountry poet, a river poet, as the poetess Alice Oswald called me in a cherished book written by her and recently sent to me. My subjects seem to pop up for me to take a shot at.

I do wonder what actually makes a poet. At the time of writing I have only met one other poet in my life. I have, though, met many people who say magical, poetical things. What I have to say is simple, sometimes at either extremes of my thoughts. At times I build my words line by line until they are a poem. Sometimes they come in a moment, sometimes they come over weeks.

I imagine a tear in the eye of a sensitive person whose life might have had a parallel experience to mine.

Someone may be given to laughter as they read my poems or may have recognised themselves doing similar things to me. If they compare my poems to themselves then so much the better. For myself I wonder who you are and I often wonder where it is you are when reading my poems?

I also use verse to express anger and disbelief at what some people would do to my ordered little world for greed and money. I resent the demise of my way of life. I think people in the regions, not just the south-west, get abused mostly because of their kindness and their love of the simple life.

For the most part I am happy when I am writing about the Westcountry and its people and its places. I do truly feel that those I love come with me. I seem to write and see with their eyes.

Anyone who has lost the one they loved and almost died themselves can only surely value life and the quality of life above anything else. I am a Fifties baby and my reflections are essentially based on the same things as anyone else of my age .The only difference is that I was lucky to be born in a beautiful place which I have rarely left. I have met many wonderful people along my life's way. What can be better, then, to set down to write and dream about those you love and have loved, in the places that you hold dear and then be able to recall those experiences?

Once again I invite you to come with me, if you will, just a little further on my journey. I like to think that my book is mostly a thoughtful, happy book that you, a good friend, are sharing. Or perhaps that you are alongside me or with the people you have chosen to love. You may be relieved, in part, of the burden of losing someone or thing that you felt an empathy with or loved when you read my poems. I truly hope so.

Most of the people I know are my friends, many of them are genuine scallywags, a little bit naughty, a little bit unpredictable and full of human failings.

Most live or have lived around the estuaries and rivers and seas of the south-west. They get by as best they can. I suspect you are no different.

I do though ask the odd question out loud when something in the world angers, shocks, puzzles or frightens me. I am not afraid to do so.

Kevin Pyne

CONTENTS

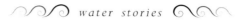 *water stories*

 *medley*

friends and scallywags

water stories

First across the Line

You might ask yourselves
Where are they gone?
Perhaps in that quiet moment
As you sit arms across the oar
Your heart pounding
Watching the sun fade from gold to red
That magic tenuous evening colour which
Never seems to stay long enough
Let then the mid blue of evening
Melt the hurt that you feel into a memory
And the warmth of shared friendship
Remind us that we are only here
For a term

Suddenly with a barked 'forward to row'
The coxswain's voice breaks the spell
You hear the pins creak
The oars swish as they cup
The green waters again and again
Until you are one with the boat
One with the crew

I wonder then will you realise
That I am beside you
My spirit forever part of the boat
I was just the first to leave
The first to cross the line
In time each of you will follow me
No crew is ever for ever
Others will sit in your place
They will touch lovingly the crafted woodwork
Laugh as you have laughed
Laugh as I laughed with you
Until only the gig remains
And our voices are lost
In the sea swell
On the out-going tide

I wrote this poem to remind rowers that they are not forever. I am honoured that good friends have used it in various ways to remember lost loved ones.

Dark girl

Oh river green as virgins eyes
Run you to the sea
Take me dark girl
Where it is I need to go
Spare no thought for me
Dark girl who runs
From the moorland's brow
So mighty and powerful
She makes flowers of great trees
Tempt me into the shimmering light
Where you make love to me

On a corner around a bend
On the stand at evening time
Where the clear fresh water
Lets in the first salt
From the great and mighty sea
That's where I sit in heaven
And heaven sits with me.

My river.

I'll see you in the islands

I'll see you in the islands when they drop the starting flag
And seven hundred rowers go to war
I'll see you in the islands when the first stroke makes her lift
And you can hear the thole pins click and strain three miles away
I'll see you in the islands when our coxswain
A mild and gentle man shouts "get out the effing way"
I see you in the islands as they row across your back
And the oars they flay and smack against her side
I'll see you in the islands when the cold Lantic ocean buries her
Rolls up above her gunwales then tries to creep inside
I'll see you in the islands as the spectacle unfolds
And brightly coloured gigs they fill the sea
I'll see you in the islands when you feel such a huge sense of pride
Knowing you're at the greatest gathering in the Westcountry
I'll see you in the islands when you know you can't go on
Yet you do, out of sheer stubbornness because you won't give in
I'll see you when your blisters start to bleed
And the coxswain whispers "give me twenty more"
I'll see you in the islands as you respond, because you're a crew
No matter how tired how wet or how sore
I'll see you in the islands when you have rowed the last hard mile
In a matter of minutes, that's of course allowing for the tide
I'll see you in the islands as you cross the finish line
Then gasp "I'm to old for this, another twenty yards
I would have died"
I'll see you in the islands as you nod and give a wave

To a fellow rower you would have murdered a little while ago
I'll see you as the cox says "row on" in a broken voice
That you can't say you've heard before and know
And I'll see you as you cross again to Saint Mary's, rowing, laughing,
light and slow
I'll see you as you lift the gig like the thoroughbred she is
Then set her square saying "gently, easy, take it slow"
I'll see you watch and clap as others receive their hard-earned medals
And pretend 'it didn't matter anyway'
I'll see you as you sing, and the songs they fill the night
Until you stagger home to bed muttering about 'giving up' along the way
I'll see you when they sing 'Trelawney'
As Chenoweth he takes the lead and the *Scillonian* leaves to pull away
I'll see you offer up a toast to anyone 'who's watching'
With a half empty can of beer
I'll hear you shout "never again" and that you can't afford it
Then I'll shout "rubbish"
Because you're a rower not a quitter and as sure as New Year follows Christmas
You'll be back again next year.

*To Joyce and Ted Gundry and anyone who has ever watched or participated in the mass
starts of pilot gigs at the World Championships weekend in the Isles of Scilly. It is in my
opinion the greatest spectacle held anywhere in the south-west.*

Thole pin is a wooden stake inserted into holes in gunwale for oars to use as a fulcrum.

Bright water light mark

Bright water light mark
Spring a tide through my mind
I'm away up the river
To see what I can find
To steal a portion of that river peace
For which I pay in kind

A silver satin bride's morn
Virginal and new
Sunlight on the windows
Glary, foxy, bright
The fields so green and shiny
Polished by the night

Let this river vagrant dream and be at peace
On this summer morning new
In among the mackerel
In among the trees
I give a little shiver
As I sneak in among the mists

Loiter in the wakening valleys
In among the new light
Crisp and apple green
Point her through the water
Clear, cold and clean

Wet assed sitting on the transom
I turn the tiller toward my dream
A wake full of shards of diamonds
For others just a dream

Penniless and happy
My old dog by my side
A nod and a laugh to an old mate as
I dodge the ferries to cross the river wide
Fat and middle-aged
And still a child of fifty-five.

To all river lovers everywhere.

Zennor hill

As I was climbing up to Zennor hill
I found a mermaid feeling ill
"Help me sir" she said to me
"I'm drying out and I need the sea
Please take me down to yonder beach
And sit me where the tide will reach
For I have sisters there to see
Five and forty we would be"
So in my arms I placed her fair
Pale her skin and bright red hair
Three fields over I did take
She to the sea for pity's sake
And as the waters touched the shore
As I heard the cold Atlantic roar
Her heart did quicken even more
Until the ocean touched her tail
Then it was as if a whale
Come up before me
There stood Father Neptune in his splendour
Came to touch his daughter tender
I bowed before this mighty king
Then the mermaids five and forty began to sing
Of a time which will come
And a time which is lost
Of pilchards, galleons and the terrible cost
They sang of the souls of the seamen gone

Last of all they sang and prayed for the poisoned sea
And the greed of mankind
That would be you and me
Who have in our greed and haste
Turned the sea to a barren waste
We have emptied it out
Taken it all
All that is left are dying dolphins
And the sad mermaids call

I like the people of Cornwall. The singsongs in the 'Tinners Arms'
in Zennor are legendary.
I love the thought of there being mermaids or as they call them down west,
merry maids.

Watching a ship on Christmas night

A ship it passed
On a Christmas night
She filled the darkness with her ports of light
Each light a cabin and which from that room
Slipped a couple I would never know
She in evening dress
He in smart new tuxedo
To take their place at table row on row
As silently to seaward she glides away
A steel village of strangers
On that Christmas day
Her great hull silhouette below a silver moon
On that cold clear night
She was gone so soon
Sliding by silently until she was out of sight
A thing of shimmering beauty
A thing of might
A Christmas tree above her
Masthead light

Out past our little harbour
Just a mile from shore
There were a thousand people
Where there were none before
All of who just sailed away
On that starlit evening
On a so still Christmas day
I watched her in the cold dark silence
Just glide away
Until her silver wake sparkled
Then spread like an angels wings
And she was gone down channel
Toward whatever it is
That tomorrow brings...

*Many years ago, when the lower Dartmouth lower ferry used to run
on Christmas day, I saw a liner off the harbour on a silver blue
beautiful calm Christmas night.*

The wind asked the river

The wind asked the river
To be loving
The wind asked the river
If it cared
The wind asked the moonlight
To be soft and blue
And to shine down
On all lovers everywhere
The wind dropped
And the stars sang
An eternal anthem to the moon
Saying we are forever
You are mortal human beings
You are all to be gone
So very soon.

Watching the Dart on a clear June night.

The great cranes

They took the great grey cranes
Those great steel herons
From the water-side
They who had stood in silent patience
Awaiting to lift their prey
In among the fires that gave birth to sea monsters
In among the arks and molten spat red white steel
They had stood in abeyance
To haul and shift for the army of oil-stained ants below
Who fettled metal into ships
The burners, the platers, the riveters
The shipwrights
Charley Weedon, Sam Elliot, Jim Chase, Les Chase
The lunchtime euchre players
Who eased the great hulls away
From the earth that bore them hence
Steel cold grey the cranes
They that did their hunting
As the wires drew away
As the cogs clanked
As the town grew prosperous
From the sums of their carriage
Until the valleys filled with the red brick
Walls of their prosperity
Now they are gone the windy guns are silent
The rails lay pitted, rusty
Never again will their gantries dip for a princess
Dip for a queen
And what is to take their place

Marina villages for quick moneyed people
Who live out their retirement
In sterile apartments
Or leave the children of those the cranes
Provided for without homes
Without hope
Easy money which pollutes and which chokes the herons
With wads of cash from the sale of things
That nobody needs
And who see no future
Beyond their greedy lives
Where are the cranes
Where is the shipyard
That spewed hundreds forth
Men who built ships
Who sensed and saw the physical results
Of their labours
Who smelt of oil and bitchmo?
As the sirens called
To bring them to work
Up at the yard
All are gone, all lost
To an age of economics
Like the ships they built
Like the communities
Like the town from which they came.

My home port was a shipbuilding port before the marinas came.

The ferryman

I'll take you up the river
Around that magic bend of dreams
To where the water stands at the tide's full time
I'll take your where the trees
Touch the spreading tide
And the summer sunshine
Shines and dances like shards of gold
I'll take you where the peace
It soaks into your mind
I'll take you to a place
Where you can feel and be yourself
And the worries of the world
Are left behind
I take you where the souls of those
That we have loved
Are free to live in peace
Forever each in their own way
I take you for an hour, one magic precious hour
So that you remember
Where you were forever on this day

I know of no better way to relax and rebuild one's mind than a river trip.
I'll take you if you like and you can see for yourself.

Something dark and dangerous

There's something dark and dangerous
It's out there not so far away
Just a little over three miles or so
Charging full tilt across the bay
Out across the bay, my friends
With her cargo loaded cheap
No one's on the helm because her captain's gone to sleep
It would be hard to keep awake you see
After all the vodka that he has drunk
Not one of her crew of Orientals knows
Or could understand
That this worn-out lonely man
Has staggered past his butt filled ash tray
And tipped into his bunk
There's no one on the helm you see
She runs on lightless and alone
The VHF is broken, the radars can't be fixed
But the fax machine from head office
Still it clicks and whirs and clicks
This monster that splits the blackness
Glides on and out of sight
As it disappears down Channel
Out into the night
For thirty years or more her filthy pitted hull
Has tramped the world around
She's destined to end up polluting
Someone else's paradise

Or split in two, broken-backed in a gale
Or hard and fast aground
Never mind her razor sharp fraying hawsers
Ignore her buckled leaking plates
Who cares just as long as there's a profit
Covered with a certificate
Of current insurance rates!
Curse the greedy shipping owners
Who pay the slaves at sea
They only care to turn another dollar
Squeeze in that one last trip
Before the breakers pay their fee
Pay as little as you can, you bastards
To the crews who man the dross
They call the coffin ships
Pray that there's no one out there fishing
As she charges on her way
'Just another mystery'
The newspaper headlines will say
'Grieving families demand answers, at ministry delay'
Wreckage indicates that all are feared lost
Leaving fisherfolk and harbour towns
As ever, picking up the human cost.

*My daughter Robyn who studies these things assures me it's only luck that there
are not more shipping disasters around our coasts.*

Spinner

He didn't go to school past puberty
He went mackerel snatching instead
Who would have cared anyway
His mother's down the pub
The old man at thirty five
Lost at sea, drowned and dead
So there's no point in crying anyway
If no one's to listen while you weep
And they say half a dozen mackerel
Buys a pasty and a fishing boat and line
It'll pay your keep
Don't go saying "how disgusting"
When he brings in the fish
Still writhing and covered over in slime
To that fancy restaurant
Wearing his dirty yellow oilers
He won't even notice you
It's just a waste of your breath and time
Because life's a bitch
And he's a fisherman
And as hard a Westcountry man
As ever you can find.

To the fishermen of the south-west - people who I say 'hello' to every day.

Paul Goddard

When I have finished this poem
It will be the thirteenth day of March
And as the sun comes up
Over the cove where pilgrims walked
And white swans raise their long necks
To take titbits from the tourists
The tourists will go on in for breakfast
Perhaps not noticing
That there is a plaque on the rounded wall
Which hides and holds the leaking tap
The plaque will read
'Paul Goddard lost at sea 12th March'
The flowers will be new
The tourists will be new and walk by
The swans will paddle off
The sun will rise up and spit its long-tongued
Silver light across the estuary
The ferry will again cross the water
And I will reflect
As others will reflect
On a young able man
Liked by everyone
Who everyone knew
And who was lost at sea
Run down they say
On the fishing vessel *Exuberance*

A well found ship
A little ship never found
Paul Goddard, a young man
Breton cap, thick socks and clipping clogs
I can hear him now
Hear him say "aye aye"
As though twenty years were yesterday
Paul Goddard who loved the sea so much
A sea which took him for its own...

I knew this man and if he had lived he would have given the world so much.

The lifeboat

Long for told and long to last
Rushing before the gale
Outward through the boiling foam
Who did I pass as I got home?
I'm a river man don't you see
I get rightly frightened by the sea
I lay safe within the harbour wall
And the seas grow ever darker tall
As the wind begins to sing
It's wrecking song
It sings "Rocks are sharp, the coast is long
Someone may die before too long"
There's the lifeboat buried in the spray
Outward bound across the bay
When all before the storm
Run the other way
Her diesel engines roar and snort
Rather she be safe in port
But there's been a report
She's buried in among the waves
The only hope for those she goes to save
Lord, keep her crewmen from their graves
Lord, the seas grow black and high
Where's the land and where's the sky?
The little lifeboat looks so small
It's a miracle that she floats at all.

To Arthur and Barbara Curnow - a couple more prominent than Berry Head.

Mid Fifties

I've moved on past my past
I'm rowing on a clear wide open sea
The sun comes up, the moon comes up
My life's in front of me
I'll never forget the things I've seen
Or the ones who have gone their way
I've come across the bitterest oceans
As I've gone on my way
Many things have snagged and pulled at me
Conspired to pull me down
And I admit quite openly
There are times when I could have
And should have drowned
There are those who for no reason
Stood to bar my path
But the time has come to lay the hurt aside
Substitute a smile and laugh
So here I am where the river is wide
And the sea like glazed diesel blue cellophane
Off to match the skills I have learnt in my life
Yes maybe get hurt again
Its time I think to chance my arm
Not hide or run away
And if anyone says to you
What do we do with a man who won't stay still
Say let him have his way.

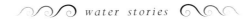
No I'm a man who needs to dream
Be alive, say what I think aloud
I not ready to fade and disappear
I'm not one for the crowd.

My independence is everything. I hope that I can be this way forever.
I've been a slave and I have served fools and paid for others' mistakes.
Now I'm fat, broke and happy!

Freewheeling down to the harbour

Freewheeling down to the harbour
On a silken summers day
Half the inshore boats are still in port
With hangovers by the way

England played on Sunday
And they all went on the booze
Worst they played and were hammered
In a game they thought they couldn't lose

Rowing my boat down the quayside
The water's like mercury
It's thick and silver
And the town so silent
I can hear the water talk to me

Watching a ship in the harbour
As she slips to get under way
She's around the bend and out to sea
Before most of the port is out of bed
On this gloriously sexy day

Look at the coloured crabbers
Look at the bright white gulls
Look at the early tickling sun
As it plays upon their hulls

Early out on the harbour
Early home for tea
Ask yourself, is there anything better
When your home's beside the sea.

My way of living is in many ways idyllic. I sense though, that it will end.

God sleeps

God sleeps in the stern sheets
Although the wind grows high
When it's rough at sea
God is there in the storm-filled sky
Even if we can't feel or see him
Even perhaps if we don't know why
Yet our God always sleeps with us
When the storms come
Under that maddened sky
God sleeps and we must trust
And hold our course
For there is fear in all things gained
And we must keep her bow true north
And trust and be guided by His hand
For we sail upon His ocean
Walk upon His land
For God is always there beside us
When we venture forth
He may not move to help us
As we start yet another day
But God sleeps in the stern sheets
Whether we are homeward or away
For each and every journey
Is never alone borne
For God sleeps in the stern sheets
To keep us safe against the storm.

I always think of my loved ones when they are away at sea.

Hulked and broken at Newlyn

Blue is the sea
She didn't lift with the tide today
She sat
Her hull rust strewn
And paint flecking, moulting
Like sea bird feathers
No strong men
Push their young knees into her gunwales
Today they came instead
With gas axes
Slodge and a swing shovel
To break her down
Pick her bones quite clean
Until she sits
Like a broken-boned whale
On the brown compacted Cornish earth
Which holds the dry
Dead stains of a little ship broken-up
Before its time.

Passing the breakers hard at Newlyn.
Nothing of beauty should be destroyed before its time.

♪♪♪ *medley* ♪♪♪

Don't go up to London

Don't go up to London, father
They'll only knock you down
Stay away down in our beloved south-west
Make them beggars come around

Don't go up to London, mother
Those streets aren't meant for us
Them lawyers in them fancy houses
They'll only steal from us

Let them search our ploughed fields
Walk our moorland ground
Let them search our creaking mine shafts
Climb our hills of clay
And when they go back to London empty-handed
We'll use our flags to wave them on their way

Don't go up to London, all you western people
Our culture must not be denied
Make them chase us out to seaward
Row back against the tide

Don't go up to London, lads and maidens
With your flags of black or green
Less'an it's for a trip to 'Twickers'
For you know what I mean!

Them city folk they'll take our houses
Insult us with their wealth
If politicians are allowed to take our flags
There'll be nothing else

No don't go up to London, cousins
They'll slaughter us again
Bring 'em down and suck 'em in
They'll not come back again

Don't go up to London, brother
Hoist your flags up far and wide
And when they see a million flags flying
Our pride in our history and our culture
Cannot be denied.

I love flags and in particular regional flags. I have always thought that the regions get seen off by central government.

Cat time

There's a cat looking at me
Through the window
Its amber eyes are wide as lights
He'll sit there until it's teatime
And the curtains are drawn for night
Then he'll find the mistress
And rub around her legs
He'll purr a tune for supper
Then he'll curl up on the floor
He'll pinch the best place on the hearth rug
As the fire starts to roar
He'll climb on you lap whilst you're sleeping
When the fire gets too hot
For every hour, on the hour
He picks the bestest spot
And when it comes to bedtime
He'll follow you upstairs
And watch you as you start to dream
And when you wake next morning
He'll be up and gone
Hunting down the garden
Where the grass is long
Whilst you cook your breakfast
And pour your first cup of tea
Just as soon as you put down a saucer of milk
Suddenly there he'll be.

To Judi Spiers who has helped me so much. A true sister to the Westcountry and its people.

Motorway theft

The biggest thief in Britain
Hides out on the motorway
Charging for tea and coffee
In the motorway services café
Yes, the toilets are much needed
And the cups and saucers clean
But the prices charged for food and drink
Are frankly bloody mean.

The cost of motorway service food takes the joy out of motorway travel.

Alfs

He plays his saxophone so sexy
That it's almost soft porn
And he belts it out for free accompanied
By a jazz guitar on a Sunday morn

The doors swing open
The doors swing closed
The music goes soft
The music goes low

Pretty friendly girls serve you dressed in black
With their midriffs bare
Their thong strings showing
And their hair tied back

Don't you just love the smell and sizzling sound?
Of bacon cooked and eggs turned 'over easy'
I do so love brown café society
It's 'so nicely sleazy'

The hot chocolate's good, the coffee's better
The fresh orange machine
Goes bang clatter clatter clatter
And weekenders and locals they chatter natter chatter

I love the pot bellied stove, I love the green
I sit and wonder at the names on the panels
Written in red in between
Don't tell me you don't love listening to half conversations over
The hissing bubbling noisy cappucino machine

All the pretty young things sit posing so nice right and neat
Such fine young bums in designer labels squeezed into tall horse drawn
Ex farm implement seats
There's a woman I know who's as cool as a fridge
Down at the café Alf Resco

A café boy in a crew shirt says
 "Hi what can I get you"
A little boy with a telescope says out loud
"Do you know that rabbits eat their own pooh"
Only at Alfies

The gates are open from seven till two
That's Wednesdays Thursdays Fridays
Saturdays Sundays too
At Alfs the huge welcome
Is always just for you

♪♪ *medley* ♪♪

The papers on the ceiling are worth a read
You might find a picture of the poet
When he was young if it's not too hard to believe
That's if you stand on your head if you ever feel the need

Alfs is a sort of inside outside
Happy chilled-out canvas shrouded manger
A café of friends they call Alf Resco
A place of welcome where no one is a stranger

Just walk in past the orange filled basket on an old grocer's bike
If you're out for a walk, if you're out for a hike
Look for the black cone charred torch above the wrought iron gates
With the lazy yellow flame at its apex burning bright

Come on in it's a favourite with me
This brown dark café that sits not far from the sea
No matter if you look casual or if you look smart
The hospitality will warm the cockles of your heart
At Alfies

Thinking of Ted, Lesley, Peter, Kate, Piers and Vince Southern (who
helped build the place).
All people who know how to 'Live, Laugh, Love' and to give a true
South Devon welcome!

Carpenter

Working with my dad
Almost drove me mad
For the learning that I had
When I was apprenticed
The old man taught me well
And as far as I can tell
He shaped me

Now my father he is gone
His trade I carry on
For I have become him
Like my father's father, I am a carpenter
Now I train another
Who is my son

I make the windows
And the chairs
The newel post and the stairs
And the coffins
When the time comes

Did not Jesus serve his trade?
To a simple man who made
The cradle where he laid
When just a baby

For in time a father becomes his son
And the boy becomes the one
Who is to be the master

I met a carpenter on a beach when antifouling my boat. This is the story he told me.

The emergency pick-you-up poem

Think of yourself as a bolt of lightning
Shooting through the blue
Think of yourself as something huge
When everything around you seems
So very small
Think of yourself as the life of the party
Even if there's no one there at all
Think of yourself as a brand new shiny flower
Grown so beautiful and tall
Think of yourself as the first one home
When everyone who loves you is away
Think to yourself then "get on with your life"
While you still have it!
Think to yourself that you owe that to
The ones who have gone away
Think to yourself that everyone loves you
Every single day
Think to yourself let's get up and at 'em
Then just blast those blues away.

Someone I love was sad one morning so I wrote this poem as a pick-you-up.

Running to school

When I was a boy
And full of spring
I used to run around everything
I used to run down to the shops
Past the hedges that lined the road
I ran and ran everywhere
Until a master at school
Said "hey you boy, you stop there"
Walk don't run is the way to go
I'll pile you up with homework
That'll make you slow
And when you have finished with me
You'll be trained up and a slave for industry
I will fill your mind
With knowledge to store
And when that's done
You'll not run any more
You'll be old and unwanted
And thrown away
A worn out cassette
From another day
So run little boy while you can
They'll steal your youth soon enough
And turn you into
A tired old man…

Education is not everything - it suits some not others.

Robert Lenkiewicz

I probably could not have spelt your name
But I can see
Oh yes I can see
I would stand in wonderment
We would stand in wonderment
And understand how you alone painted for a generation
How you take from water its shimmering seductive soul
Encapsulate it in haze and mists
Yellow blue bold oils
Yet you understand
That a beautiful young girl is beautiful
You leave her tempting
Embayed in her first rush of womanhood
Long after it would have been stolen
By drink, drugs, motherhood
Beatings
Dark is dark, so dark
Light is light, such wild light
In a darkened room
As colour grows
Conducted age on age
Until it says
How it says
If you look you will see the truth

Unclean unpolished truth
And be warned
You will be uneasy
With its latent sexual energy
The colours and contours of death proclaimed
Yellow, blue, there is so much blue in death
It is etched into their faces
In the stories that no one else bothered to ask
I should have asked you to paint her
You frightened me in some way
And I wondered would she be safe
Naked
Her hair red
Her skin so pale
I should have asked while she lived
She would have smiled then

Forever…

*My late wife and my first trips together, to Plymouth, coincided with
Lenkiewicz's first outdoor murals. She was comfy with her body. I doubt she
would have minded.*

My dad's old army beret

I lost my dad's old army beret
When I was in a younger mind
I didn't realise the value in it
As it was from another time
Another time when the world went crazy
Then tried to kill itself
And me I took the only thing
That he kept to remind him
I just saw it tucked up on the shelf
I was just a thoughtless trendy youngster
When parkas and army surplus were all the rage
We wore the bits that men wore to war
When they where just a little over our age
We wore them without thinking
Of those men who dressed in those clothes with pride
We were young then and so full of life
None of our friends had died
So I pinched the old man's maroon beret
And with all my mates went out
I left it on the bus that night
When we kids were skylarking about
I tried to go and find it
But it was already gone

Only when I grew to be a man
Did I realised I shouldn't have put that beret on
Because it was the beret of my father, a soldier
Earned in a world war
I had lost what five years cost
And time could not renew
That beret was a thing of pride for a man to wear
Worn before I was born
By a man who went to battle
Not a thing a boy should have worn
My father wore that beret with millions of others
To keep the black poisoned tide at bay
If I could have one wish
I would wish
He could have gone on wearing it
Until this very day…

My dad and I never seemed to hit it off. I have been lucky with my kids. I wish it could have been the same. War takes so much out of so many.

Jeans

I'm an old rocker
And I'll always dress that way
Denim shirt and a pair of Levis
Is for me
Forever the rig of the day
The kids may laugh if they want to
But I don't give a toss
I pay the bills
And as long as they live under my roof
Father is the boss
Yes I'm an old rocker I dress in sixties gear
And I'm not going to give it up
Now that old age draws near
It was good old James Taylor
Who dressed at first this way
When he first sang 'Fire and Rain'
As Susanne she went away
I told your shivering mother
That I loved her
Barefoot after a midnight swim
She was wrapped around in my denim shirt
Wearing a pair of my jeans
Can you believe your fat old dad
Was once a lover
Once so young and thin?

My children actually can see that I do have a life.

53

Alfred and me

Me and Alfred Wallis
Were very much the same
They said he couldn't paint for toffee
And I can't spell his name
So old Alfred kept on painting
He didn't know the rules
Alfred is a now a member
Of the famous Newlyn school
He paid for bread with pictures
The baker's wife down in Saint Ives
Thought it was a swindle
And she the foolish woman that she was
Used them in the ovens
To supplement her kindle
Now his pictures sell for thousands
And hang in all the galleries
I wonder if someone then
Would give me ten quid
For a book of poetry

I am in many ways the last person to be a poet. I can't spell and my punctuation is awful. As they say 'if it flies, fly it'!

Tee-shirts

I am wearing a brand new tee-shirt
For the very first time today
It says I've been there, seen it, done it
Gone on out and won it
Had a trip around some foreign bay
I'm wearing a brand new tee-shirt
And I only wish one thing
That my ageing fat sagging tummy
Was a six-pack
And that I could remember
When you used to sleep in my tee-shirts
And I was young, flat, hard and slim.

The older man's lament - well for me anyway.

Schooldays

I'm the kid from the back of the class
Grubby shirt and muddy ass
I'm the one who didn't understand
Punctuation or Shakespeare grand
I'm the one who was left behind
I'm the one who found it hard to find
His place
As the other kids were streamed
I'm the one who sat and dreamed
Even bullyboy Hickey screamed detention
Never served to steal my attention
For far beyond those white-bloused catholic girls
Runs a river through my mind
Runs a heart they'll never find
I've seen them since in shiny cars
Tiny houses, Wonderbras
Played out cassettes before their time
Thanks so much
I'm doing fine
Mea culpa, Mea culpa, Mea maxima culpa.

My Catholic upbringing was not always such a good thing. Some things make me feel guilty and I think that is why I write poetry. At times it is a way of being a confession.

Ice house

Father and mother were strangers
When father came back from the war
How could he understand her new independence?
She the things that he saw

I was just a product of a lost wish
That sailed in on the tide of the forlorn
They tried to regain their lost love
And after a last night of lust
Like thousands of others I was born

They looked at each other like leopards
And snarled any time they were close
I wonder if they ever realised
That it was me that they hurt the most

How could they tell me they loved me
When each of them had forgotten
In that ice house what was love for
All I ever remember is them shouting
As I slid back out left by the back door

My parents they hated each other
Of this I am really quite sure
Two strangers who lived in the same house
The physical products of war

Me I am Fifties baby born out of love far too late
My sole reason for being was almost
To fill up the third bedroom
On a brand new housing estate

There were hundreds of kids who had no one to love them
Small wonder that we in the Sixties went daft
Who found hundreds of young people just like us
All eager to have fun love explore and to laugh

We tried lots of things that we shouldn't
Questioned and found our own way
But most of all we promised ourselves
We would learn just how to love
And never live in our parents way

We brought up our children and loved them
Like no other children before
The kids from the mad generation
Whose grandparents gave up their love to make war.

I felt my parents couldn't show their love for me.

Growing up

Don't grow up too soon
There's a life beyond the moon
Take your time to be on your way
Wait another day
Growing up comes so soon
And you'll sing an older tune
Soon enough
Take your time to leave
Don't let impatience thieve
From you your childhood
It's okay to go away
Just leave it another day
And go when you want to
Remember then the hardwood tree
Which takes such a long time
To seed, to be
That it stands for an eternity
I know you have to go
Just take it nice and slow
And when you decide to go
Just take it steady
Be safe, be prepared
Be happy with yourself
Be ready.

To Christina T, a river friend and person I watched growing up.

Joe Mugford

Joe Mugford
Was madder then a rabid dog
As thick around as a floating log
And when a full moon on its way
All along the quay Joe would sway
Shouting "Torbay crab"
Joe always shouted never talked
He even directed cars under the Butterwalk
(Silly buggers some of these tourists)
All the towns' folk said
"Look out, Joe's a-coming"
As he spluttered muttered humming
"Torbay crab"
I heard the pail with crabs a-strumming
As they tried to escape their fate
And pre-empt that fateful date
With boiling water
Winter long and summer green
In peaked cap and old grey rain coat of gaberdine
They say he was a gunner on a submarine
Got forgotten as the sub went down
Left poor old Joe to swim or drown
He got washed off a clipper ship
Rounding the Horn on the outward trip
Got washed back on the other side
Held up his seaman's book with pride
To prove he was a Cape Horner

Got one over on Bob Griffiths the harbour master
Told a whopper, bigger, faster
Old Joe was silent until the moon was high
Then he shouted at the passers by
"Torbay crab "
As through the town he did his rounds
"Torbay crab"
To that lovely reverberating sound
Of a galvanised pail
Dropped onto the pavement
Set down when he held court noisily
Two octaves below timpani
In our little town beside the sea
Whilst all the old boys gathered around
Noting that Joe was back in town
Joe would splice and spice up any day
He's dead now and long time gone away
I think of him when the moon is high
And the old boys sitting by
The boat float
Tom Blamey, Uncle Jack Riddles, Fred Peachy
Bob Griffiths one and all
Men turned boys again, sitting in the sun
Above the green and slimy boat float wall.

This was the town of my boyhood. I have always wished he would have shouted
"Start Bay crab" but he didn't.

On the beach at Mount's Bay

I stood on the shore with a Cornishman
And as we talked
Our thoughts went out to sea
We talked as men would talk
And of things which ought to be
We talked of the loss of the herring
We talked of the loss of our homes
And we talked of the man from up country
That picked and sold our bones
We talked of tall strong miners
Whose hands grew soft and pale
And we talked of those who
Would make us take down our flags
Said "we would rather go to jail"
We talked of the honest farmer
His cattle sold and gone
And all those redundant farm yards
Who have four tracks parked upon

"Is it a crime" my friend said "to only want enough"?
Is it a crime to only want to pull together?
Not to think of money and other stuff
There's many a rich man died around here
When the seas are getting rough
"You see "said the Cornish man
With a wry dry Cornish smile

"They may take our houses
They may have more money then we
But they will never be Westcountry men
They are not children of the sea
The tide can't rise in their arteries
The sun don't set in their eyes
And they can't see the names of their loved ones
When the storm clouds are written in the skies
All the money in the High Street
Unless it's brought here in a pram
Wouldn't up and make you for one ounce
A true Westcountry man."

Time to talk treason I think.

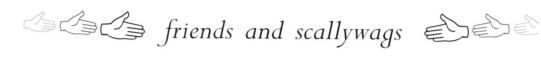

friends and scallywags

Friends and scallywags

I wish you a blue tide in the morning
And warmth in your heart from the sun
I would ask that you start every day without malice
That you treat each day as the first and only one
I would wish that you see forever in your mind's eye
Our harbour in all its beauty in the first light
Or as it turns blue under a shining silken silver moon
And that you hold this vision of the home of your childhood
Wherever it is that you be
As the stars which make up your birth sign
Sparkle like fireflies over our river as it runs away to the sea
Keep a place just then in your heart at this moment
And remember your mother and me
I wish you long strong friendships
With those whose mothers and fathers who were children
When I was a child and who played and ran alongside me
We were such friends and scallywags then
As I hope you and the friends of your generation
Will by then have turned out to be
I wish you the freedom to do as you wish
Not become a keeper or broker to fools
And I ask that you abide by what is right
Not be swallowed up by modern jargon or by stupid petty rules
Don't make or deal in false promises
For we stand and fall by our word
I wish you grace in all things

At the right time when it's appropriate that you care
I don't wish you a mountain of riches
All that I ask is that you remain honest and fair
Remember and ask yourself "would it be right?"
When those who brought you up can no longer guide you
Because they are no longer there
I wish you a smile in your mind and the knowledge
That those you chose to love, love you
And that they remain safe even when you are elsewhere
I wish you the courage to say "no"
And a path you can walk with others as well as yourself
That you fill your days with worthwhile distance
Enjoy the journey outward as much as the long journey home
I expect that you should help those who need help
As you go on and make your own way
Don't always look for profit
Sometimes in life there is no profit to pay
Instead I wish you good luck and the trust of strangers
Topped up with laughter that lasts the whole day
I wish you the ability to remain yourself
Whilst not being selfish
That you give your all to the game
If you are agreeable to play
Keep company with those friends who are scallywags
They're the best kind of people you see
They are the friends of your's and my youth

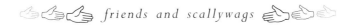

They are people we love the most
They are the people of the sea
It has nothing to do with creed, religion or skin colour
They are the people who have in their hearts
Our beloved Westcountry.

For the greater part this poem was written in hospital. I was not actually sure if I had a future at the time.
My children had already lost their mum. I came across it again recently and I still stand by what I wrote then.

The painting

She stepped down from the train
Walked into the picture
Stepping over and into the frame
On that late summer's day
So she smiled as she always smiled
Her amber hair like jewellery
As she passed by a fisherman
Stopped for a moment to ask him the way
In the last summer light
In her heart it felt so very right
As she smiled at a ferryman
Who came the other way
He had never met a woman such
He knew right away he would love her much
She liked what she saw so she decided to stay
As they talked in the evening light
She told him it would be all right
So he asked if she would
She said that she thought she could
And right away they understood
And made love all that long night
They filled up the picture
With a dog and kids and happiness
She left, as he knew she would
In a chest made of coffin wood
Leaving the picture on a late September day

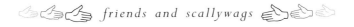

But the picture is the picture
It's always just as colourful
Save for the ferryman who sits on his own now
Never regretting or wondering why or how
In the warm sunshine.

Lyzie always said that her first sight of Dartmouth
was like walking into a painting.

A prize worth having

They came together almost reticent
She a little shy
Simply anxious to please
But they had agreed
And others had warned him
That this would be the case
He had wanted to try her
For himself
Having heard she could be very good
If helped at the beginning
So they came together
For this purpose
And only once
So it had to be right
She was anxious
Almost timid
But they had no time
This was to be it
Just the once
Expecting too much too quickly
He snarled at her
To his surprise
She snarled back
You see they had no time
It was just this once
And it had to be right

Quickly they realised
If they did it together
Each for each other
And only the once
It could be good
It had to be good
His performance had to match others
Remembering kindness
Through the adrenaline rush
And having no other recourse
He muttered encouragement paid her a compliment
She responded to him right away
She gave him her all
He could not believe how someone so small
Could give of so much
Realising almost in panic that his performance
Would have to match hers
Beads of sweat began to cover them both
Could they go on and on
Faster and faster
With a rhythm perfectly in time
Successful
Enjoying their success
Having even time for a whispered word
She felt his strengths
He knew that what he had heard about her was true

She was very very good
They were soaked to the skin
Neither of them caring
They could go on and on
Until a huge bang
Left them spent
Suddenly brought them earthwards
It was over
The regatta was theirs
They had won the mixed pairs

I feel very strongly that women rowers are much underrated and yet many are superb and are always less trouble then men.

Elwyn

What can I do with Elwyn?
He's my oldest mate
He was a boy when I was a boy
I guess it's just too late

What can I do with Elwyn?
He has such a cheeky grin
He's still pulling the girls half his age
Though married twice he's been

What can you do with Elwyn?
Who arrives half-pissed for tea
Then tucks the table cloth in his trousers
And gets up walks away and breaks
Your Dartington crystal and all your crockery

What can you do with Elwyn?
Who arrives naked at your door?
Whose BMW although brand new is five colours
Is bent and broken and won't go any more

What can you do with Elwyn?
With his naughty smile and all those chat-up lines
No need to any thing about Elwyn
Elwyn's doing fine.

My life-long friend and local hell-raiser.

73

Autumn

There was to be no autumn
In our lives
The summer fruits were gathered in
The harvest safe
Warmth and comfort we had in plenty
Autumn never came
The table was set
You left before the feast
All through the lean years we toiled together
Our only payment, love
Our reward, children
Years that passed so quickly
They are grown so strong, so beautiful
Yet they are robbed
As we are cruelly robbed
We will be strong for each other
We loved and laughed at the same things
You have though left us in a family
And again in distant time
There will be autumn in our lives

It always seems to me to be a bitter irony when people die young.

The sea in her hand

She holds the sea in her hand
For only a moment
The white foam hisses
Disappears through her fingers
Invites the primaeval
To take again control
As the white foam clears
Its power demands that she follow
Into the sea
Descending again between her fingers
Through the channels of her lifeline
Into the jade green mass
Of a dreamer's mystery
She stares at the cold clear sea
Then dives cleanly into the under life
Leaving barely a ripple
In the reflections of the summer light
To meet again some part of her mind
Left in her childhood
Lost from time's first day
She swims in the sea
As she did when a child
Again her eyes are open beneath the waves
As she feels the deep's mysteries
Feels the pulse of the earth
Take her and lift her up

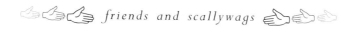

In the secret half light
Which consumes again her mind
She swims in the sea
Beyond care, beyond thought
As she slips again into the elements
Of a childhood spent this way.

Thinking of my daughter Robyn swimming.
She used to say "Daddy I have to go swimming I'm drying out"
I have never known anyone more at home in or on the sea.

Naked nude at Slapton

It was midnight
We went swimming in the sea
We all said "what the hell"
"Let's party"
What would be would be
The girls were young and firm then
The boys were tall and strong
There was no reason to hide our bits
Or put anything on
Naked, young and believing
That we would last forever
Or so it seemed back then
Naked, young and laughing
Swimming in the sea
I remember asking for my lighter
She stood there wet, redheaded and naked
Like a merry maid in the sea
She held her cold pale breasts
Against my chest as she shivered
Clinging on to me
Then she kissed me
Blue eyed and mouth wide open
And after a while said "darling, smoking is bad for you,
I have no lighter, can't you see"

We raised hell when we were young -

I wonder how many parents were just the same back then?

Julie

I watched a feather floating down
I tried to hold it, catch it so
Yet every time I reached for it
The wind would surely blow

The wind it took my love away
Without a reason why
Until just as that soft light feather
Touched the lush green grass
She turned into a butterfly

I tried to cup that butterfly
To take it in my hand
But just as I reached out to her
She flew away from me

How could anyone not help but fall in love
With such a fragile thing
Perhaps in time I'll be with feather
Perhaps in time I'll take wing

And when a feather I become
The wind will blow me so
Until I'm higher then a steeple top
Still up and up I'll go

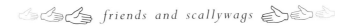

Again I'll find my butterfly
I'll blow a kiss across her soft warm wings
And she will turn into the woman I loved
That special magic being

And she will smile that special smile
Which I have longed so long to see
And she will laugh her very special laugh
And fly away with me...

Julie died from cancer. I barely knew her but her smile
reminded me of someone I once liked.

Heart

You know where my heart is
It's in between the waves
It has no headstone set to drown it
It has no earthly grave
It's flying like a white gull
In the blue sky
On a summer's day
It's playing like the dolphins
Wherever they may be
It's in the rising ball of sun
That spreads across the mighty sea

You know where my heart is
Although it can't be found
It flies up with the storm winds
It beats with passion deep within that sound
You know where my heart is
It beats softly right next to you
It's hidden in among the autumn river mists
Right there in among the dew
You know where my heart is
Because it was once yours to take
Even though I'm gone from you
It's still yours forever's sake.

To all my friends who live on the Yealm - especially the Leonards and Lizzie Stone.

February 14th 1985

You hit me with a pillow
I threw a rolled up sock
You tipped the dregs
Of a cold tea cup
Down my warm back
And ran off naked
That was a bit of a shock

I wrote across your bum
'Valentine I love you'
With a bright red lip stick pen
You said the kids aren't back till four
The day is ours till then

You said "where is my card"?
I said "what card"?
I smiled as in fact I sent you two
One I addressed from a secret admirer
Just to see what you would do

You ran off in my shirt
When you heard the postie come
You looked so fresh and sexy
I had to remind myself
You were someone's mum

Well you weren't daft
And quickly guessed it
You laughed and said "that it was me"
I wanted to know I could trust you
I just wanted to see
I felt relieved and happy
Until you smiled and said
That in fact you had received three

My heart it stopped for a moment
It missed the very next beat
Until you showed me the card
Which one of our kids had drawn
And said "that'll teach you"

I was the victim of my deceit.

Happy times: I would wish everyone to be happy at least once in their lives.

Black smooth jade

You gentle soft spoken Celtic women
I love you so much
I just like the softness in your voices
Like smooth black jade
I just love to watch you
I have no need to touch
I will respect and honour you
Drink from the smiles you give
I am not a man to be underhand
Just happy that I live
To feast of plenty
Upon your friendship
Is all I truly need
For in your pride and gentle kindness
Grows a golden seed
And I will write in praise of you
Until the last sun sets low
Over those spoils of china clay
And great black shadows grow
And I will love your Celtic features
Forever plus one day
Or I can walk through Lyonnesse to Scilly
Or St Piran comes again your way

*To my Cornish friends Bev and Lins. People with whom
I have travelled across creeks and oceans.*

My friend Caroline

Its either sunflowers
Or land mines
And I am never sure
Which
Even on a beautiful day
As I walk in the garden of kindness
Which is my friend
There will be hidden among the sunflowers
A land mine
No matter how beautiful
She can be very beautiful
One misplaced step
Can cause such an explosion
That the garden disappears
Into a brown barren rage
But I like the garden
It fascinates, intrigues me
I still want to walk in the garden
Please could you erect a sign
So that I understand
When and when not the garden is open
Could it read
'Danger Landmine
Exploding Caroline'…

I think so much of this lady - it may not seem so but I truly do.

Amy unusual

She hones her words
Steel stainless sharp words
From a young sharp latent deliberate mind
Slow stone honed words of deep cutting excellence
Each word is bought at such a price
She saves herself for her words
She is a slave to her every line
She drags them
And piles them up
They are lines which are so frail
They would topple
As if toy bricks
Line on line
She spins them up and up
Until she can live out her life
Within them
If she were rushed
They would be lost
If she were startled
They would take flight and fall away
They must be drawn from her
Gathered up
Like fine spun silk
How is it I wonder
That such a talent goes unrecognised
That she has no proclamation

To go before her
As she disappears
At the end of class
To a dream which she shares
With no one.

On meeting Amy Robinson, a very deep talented inner city poet in Plymouth, at a reading of my poems.

Sue and Jane

Sue and Jane
On the old man's Honda
White blondes
On an early summer's day
Arms around each other
Staring seaward silent miles away
Both their mother's daughters
Long and beautiful
Never more beautiful than that day
I felt embarrassed to disturb them
It was one of those life's moments
That a man may never see
Two beautiful sisters
An insight into womanhood
Lost and in love with each other
Oblivious to me
For just that one lost moment
On that little ferry by the sea.

*Sue and Jane Poyser sisters, beautiful girls who crossed the
Dartmouth lower ferry so very many times until they went
away to pursue careers and raise families of their own.*

Two Valentines

"Come sit on the bed" you said
"I need to talk to you
I know you love me" you said
"I know you have always been true"

"You won't survive alone
So please for me don't try
And for a time my darling
There will be no Valentine
Life will pass you by"

"Those blue eyes and that little boy's smile
Will bring someone to you
Don't say no, just let go
That's all you'll have to do"

"I promise you in time, my darling
You will be someone else's Valentine
There'll be someone else for you
Someone else will hold your heart
Keep you straight and true"

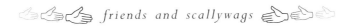

I know you have always loved me
And I know for the time I have left
That you are mine
I love you, I am releasing you from our vows
To be one day
Someone else's Valentine"

"In time you will bring her flowers
She will laugh with you
And instead of one love
Who shared in your life
You will be a lucky man
A man who can say
That he has had two".

My late wife Lyzie sat me on the bed in hospital and told me this.
Wherever did she draw her strengths from at such an awful time I wonder?

Lyzie

She simply left
As I always knew she would leave
This the price I would have to pay
I knew from the beginning
It would not, could not last forever
No one thing could be so beautiful
So calm
As summer seas are calm
I loved you but I understood
You had to go
I can never think of you without smiling
And I love to say your name
With your hair still as red as late September sunsets
You left
Before the winter came
A merry maid
Who went back into the water
I know where you are
Just a little further up the river

I like to think that my lovely Lyzie is always
around me; to look at my daughter Robyn is to know this.

A poem for the broken-hearted

Until the tears of loss
Cross and fall in channels of sorrow
From your face
There can be no end to sadness
Shedding those tears is the first step
As you move away
When we remember
Those who are gone
Remember now they are gone forever
It is the way
So let those tears come and fall
They will mend the hurt
Those warm clear salted waters
Will in time mend the loss
The sorrow will turn to daylight
The pain will ease
But it takes time
So much painful time

For anyone who has suffered great loss.

INDEX

93

ACKNOWLEDGEMENTS

My thanks go out to the following.

Little has changed in this, my second book. I thank the people that cross in and out of my life. I hope they always will.

I thank Clare Thorp together with her daughter Christina for initially checking my spellings. Clare has understood and helped me in so many ways. It's an odd thing watching her daughter Christina, a very intelligent young woman who is still in full time education, sitting in school uniform checking and correcting my awful spelling.

Thanks to my daughter Robyn, so like her mum that my lovely Lyzie will always be around (even though I am learning to tuck her away slowly). I wing poems across to Robyn over the internet and she always has time to read them and send them back, sometimes when they must stir deep emotions in someone so young.

If it were not for my son Ross there would be no book I lost the first draft of these poems into cyber-space recently - luckily he was able to retrieve them yet again.

My thanks to Richard and Gilly Webb for helping me and being so patient. Richard is a Westcountryman first, last and always. I feel that my writings are not just a book of poems to him. Richard puts far more time into my poems then ever his reward as a publisher justifies. Richard and Gilly are busy people, yet they find time for so many things.

My thanks also go to Laurence Daeche for his excellent design work on both my first and this my second book of poems.

I would want to thank by name Bev Davis and Lindsey Bryning, two good Cornish sister friends for reading the first draft of this book of poems. Bev and Lins had previously kindly taken the time read the draft of my first book whilst we were on the Isles of Scilly a year previously. I think I need their Celtic blessings - it's become a good luck thing. Supper in that island bistro was such a laugh. I will never see a French stick without thinking of you both.

Maggie Trubshaw, Sarah Flint, Lizzie Busby, Jane Naish, all need to be thanked for either helping me or allowing themselves to be my subject matter.

I also wish to thank those people who took the time to review my first book and who gave me the encouragement to carry on.

I thank the TV and radio presenter Judi Spiers from the bottom of my heart for her help. She has been wonderful. So indeed have Andréa and the staff in the Harbour Bookshop here in Dartmouth. Without all of their collective energy would I would never have got this far.

Thank you again to all those strong ladies who slip into and out of my life. I need and care for all of you. I have some strong wonderful women friends. I truly do and especially Clare.

Finally and importantly it means so much to me when people approach me and say that they enjoyed a sentiment or identified with a line from one of my poems It really does. Please don't stop! You are one of my key sources of inspiration.

Kevin Pyne

I took the photograph illustrated on the front cover showing the beautiful locally built pilot gig Leander kindly loaned by Britannia Royal Naval College, Dartmouth to Dart Gig Club Ladies at the World Pilot Gig championships in the Isles of Scilly (chosen as it has three people dear to me in it).

Clare Thorp took the photographs of me and my family!

95

Praise for *Further up the River* by Kevin Pyne (2004)

"Kevin Pyne's poems are powerful and original, his images unexpected and perceptive. He evokes with equal tenderness his love for his dead wife and his love of the river and the sea. I believe anyone who reads them will be both touched and profoundly moved by his passion."
David Dimbleby

"I recommend these poems above all to anyone who wants to do more than blow through a place, anyone who has time to sit down and listen a little more deeply to one of the west's true voices."
Alice Oswald, *Winner of the 2002 T.S. Eliot Prize*

"This is a book of tough unsentimental poems ...an astonishing success in countryside publishing."
Bill Taylor, *Editor, Countryman*

"A beautiful celebration of Westcountry life... a tonic for anyone with preconceptions about the world of poetry, the book is quite simply devoid of pretension."
Vicky Sartain, *Devon Today*

"A perfect read...the poems are powerful and original and are written with a deep understanding of his work, love and the Westcountry."
Devon Life

"I didn't make it to the end of the first poem. I had to put the book down because the tears were blinding me...this (is a) compassionate work of art..."
Bob Curtis, *Herald Express*

"A must for your bookshelf."
Hilary Bastone, *Herald Express*

"Undoubted ability to put his words into powerful and perceptive poetry..."
Colin Bradley, *Western Morning News*

"I have read and re-read the poems. I imagine I will be doing so for many years to come. They are a source of great enjoyment."
Jude Chilvers, *Sunday Independent*

"I haven't lost the love of my life, I don't have a long and passionate history with the coves and waterways of the river Dart, I don't row and I don't have children...that was until I read Kevin Pyne's poetry and then I'm right there with him, feeling everything he feels, seeing it all through his eyes."
Judi Spiers